how to be a
bridesmaid

how to be a
bridesmaid

Amy Elliott

with photography by Winfried Heinze

RYLAND
PETERS
& SMALL

LONDON NEW YORK

Senior Designer Sonya Nathoo
Commissioning Editor Miriam Hyslop
Location Researcher Emily Westlake
Production Gemma Moules
Publishing Director Alison Starling

Stylist Liz Belton
Illustrator Robyn Neild

First published in the United States
in 2007 by Ryland Peters & Small, Inc.
519 Broadway, 5th Floor
New York, NY 10012
www.rylandpeters.com

10 9 8 7 6 5 4 3 2 1

ISBN-13: 978 1 84597 399 5
ISBN-10: 1 84597 399 2
Printed in China

contents

introduction

If you're reading this, a woman very close to you has asked you to participate in her wedding. You're excited. You're picturing yourself clad in a baby blue taffeta dress…shedding tears during the bride's vows…linking arms with a cute groomsman… But agreeing to be a bridesmaid is not a one-day-only commitment. Now, you may have heard that…

Bridesmaids wear many hats.
You can definitely expect to play the role of party planner, fashion stylist, cheerleader, even that of psychotherapist.

Being a bridesmaid is expensive.
It is—but what can you do, really? Try to take heart in the knowledge that the bride will return the favor when it's your turn to tie the knot.

Bridesmaids are forced to wear hideous dresses.

Not true! Movies often like to portray bridesmaids wearing tacky, over-the-top dresses for comic effect, but never fear—today's bridesmaid attire takes its cue from the ready-to-wear catwalk.

Being a bridesmaid is stressful.

Emotions run high when planning a wedding, and as a member of the bride's intimate circle, yes, you may encounter a few sticky situations with your cohorts, or even the bride herself. But you'll eventually laugh at all the "drama" (and besides, your experience may well be drama-free).

So what will it be like for you? Every bridesmaid's experience is different, of course, but all the basics are covered in this little handbook. It will keep you informed—and sane—every step of the way. So, let's get started!

an ancient tradition

As a bridesmaid, you are participating in a marriage tradition that has endured for thousands and thousands of years. In Ancient Greece, the matriarchs of a community would escort a new bride to her nuptials. Since the bride was often very young, these mature women were there to offer her comfort and support on the day of the wedding. Later, they would continue to guide and educate her as she transitioned into her new role of wife.

The custom of bridesmaids dressing alike can be traced back to the Middle Ages, when brides were sometimes kidnapped en route to their nuptials, either by a jealous suitor, a robber who hoped to make off with her dowry, or the groom himself. Wearing similar outfits, these early bridesmaids would

cluster around the bride as she made her way to the wedding, ostensibly to confuse potential assailants. In some circles, the goal was to repel the evil eye—bridesmaids would dress in attire almost identical to the bride so that any malevolent forces that wished to cause harm would not know which maiden was getting married.

At her 1953 wedding to JFK, Jackie Kennedy had 10 bridesmaids who wore gowns of shocking pink silk.

Selecting a maid of honor also finds its roots in the conventions of the Middle Ages, when witnesses were required to confirm that neither the bride nor the groom were marrying against his or her will. The bride would extend this "honor" to her sister or best friend. Today, the maid of honor is still set apart from the rest of the party and fulfills special responsibilities.

your duties

general duties

The official "duties" of a bridesmaid come down to a combination of tasks, time commitments, and financial responsibilities. A typical bridesmaid's participation involves helping to plan the bridal shower and bachelorette party, attending bridesmaid dress-shopping appointments, and assisting the bride with minor tasks, such as stuffing and sealing invitations, tying ribbons and tags to favors, compiling welcome baskets for out-of-town guests, or even driving one of the bride's relatives to the airport. She also provides advice, creative input, and emotional support on an ongoing basis, and is there to troubleshoot any day of the wedding disasters—say, retrieving a veil that was left accidentally at the bride's apartment, or tracking down the make-up artist when she's thirty minutes late.

In general, you will be expected to pay for

* Your bridesmaid dress and any necessary alterations
* Shoes
* Accessories
* Your accommodation and travel costs

busy, busy!

In the months preceding the wedding, you can expect to have a very active social calendar. There are many ancillary celebrations that surround the wedding itself, and all members of the bridal party are expected to free their schedules to attend them. These events might include:

* The couple's engagement party
* A shower for the bride
* A bachelorette party
* A rehearsal dinner the night before the wedding
* A farewell brunch the day after the wedding

Other time commitments you need to account for are bridesmaid dress-shopping (one or two Saturday afternoons, perhaps) and your dress fittings (scheduled at your convenience—count on at least one, if not two).

extra credit

In addition to fulfilling your regular duties, you might like to treat the bride to a few extra-helpful gestures and heartwarming surprises that go above and beyond what's normally expected of bridesmaids. Of course, every girl's time commitments and financial situation are different, but if you find that you have extra room in your schedule (and wallet), there's no limit to the ways in which you can be of assistance to the bride. To make her experience all the more special, consider:

* Pre-addressing the envelopes of the bride's bridal shower thank-you notes
* Creating and maintaining a scrapbook/photo album that chronicles all the moments and events that occur during the run-up to her wedding
* Packing an "emergency kit" to keep on hand throughout the day, especially when the bride's getting dressed. Include items like extra bobby pins, an emery board, double-stick tape, aspirin, antacid, and a needle and thread
* Placing flowers in the couple's honeymoon suite, along with snacks and a chilled bottle of champagne

*Brides always thank
their bridesmaids with
a lovely gift.*

maid of honor's duties

If a bride has assigned you the role of maid or matron of honor, you are her primary source of emotional support should she encounter a stressful situation or need help making a difficult planning decision. You are also "captain" of the crew—it's your job to manage the other bridesmaids, informing them of important dates, fielding logistical questions, and delegating tasks. In addition to your managerial role, you must also uphold your basic bridesmaid responsibilities, as well as those that are exclusively the maid of honor's domain. Traditionally, she

* Precedes the bride in the processional (if there are no children in the wedding)
* Arranges the bride's train when she reaches the altar (and bustles it for the reception)
* Holds the groom's wedding band during the ceremony
* Holds the bride's bouquet during the vow exchange
* Signs the marriage license as a witness
* Makes a toast at the reception (optional, but a nice gesture—why should the best man get all the glory?)

The bride's sister is often chosen to be the maid or matron of honor. A close friend may also take on this role.

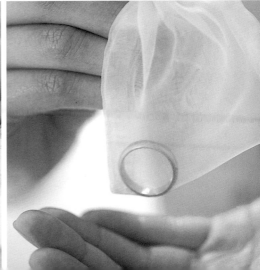

your dress

shop talk

Bridesmaids are always the best-dressed guests at the party.

The color, length, and style of the bridesmaid dress is ultimately the bride's decision, which will most likely depend on her personal taste, as well the time of year, the time of day, and the formality of the wedding. Hopefully she will also take into account what you and the other girls in the bridal party can reasonably afford to spend on the dress, as well as the degree to which the hue and silhouette suits you!

Many brides kindly allow their bridesmaids some input and you may spend a weekend or two shopping for dresses as a team. If a joint shopping trip isn't possible, discussions can take place via email—almost every designer will have photos of dress styles posted online; you can email your favorites to each other until you reach a unanimous decision. To save time (or if reaching a unanimous decision seems unrealistic), many brides simply choose a dress they like and will

notify you of the designer, style number, and color. In this case, you're expected to order the specified dress, in your size, through your local bridal salon. While this system may seem a bit bossy and self-centered, it's actually the most efficient way to handle the choosing-a-dress situation, especially if you and the other bridesmaids live in different cities.

Many brides request that their bridesmaids wear specific shoes, too. Black pumps or strappy sandals are a popular choice, you might also suggest gold or silver leather as an option—anything but dyed-to-match satin! And the style and components of the bouquet you carry will also be the bride's decision.

On the other hand, your bride may be very laissez-faire, giving very general guidelines ("any long black dress" or "a flowered sundress") so that each of you may wear a dress of your own choosing. Whatever scenario you encounter, be prepared, be a good sport, and keep in mind that the bridesmaids are always the best-dressed guests at the party.

flying colors

When discussions about dress color come up, your bride may look to you for suggestions. To begin, remind her that dark colors are more slimming than pastels and that solid colors are more forgiving than stripes, plaid, or prints (though it's perfectly okay—and quite pretty—to incorporate a sash in a contrasting hue). Also consider the season: Rich navy, claret, chocolate-brown, and plum will go off well in the context of a fall or winter wedding (you might also try ice-blue or silver). Alternatively, shades of preppy pink, custard, or periwinkle can be gorgeous at a summer garden party.

When trying to choose a color that will suit a group with different skin tones, finding a hue that's universally flattering is essential. Many bridal parties have had luck with mint-green, celadon, and sage, colors that retain their beauty on almost everyone. The same is true of "medium" pinks. As a rule, colors with a bit of complexity are more successful than straightforward "primary" hues. So instead of bright scarlet, choose a red with brown or burgundy undertones. Lilac is a nice, versatile color because it can skew pink or lavender, depending on how fair or dark you are.

choosing a style

When choosing a bridesmaid dress that will suit a group of girls with different body types, remember that V-necks are universally flattering, as are scoop necklines, and empire waists. Here are more specific guidelines:

① *flabby arms*

TRY Long or three-quarter-length sleeves. Consider wearing a shrug or wrap.
AVOID Sleeveless and off-the-shoulder styles.

② *petite figure*

TRY Tailored sheaths, or modest A-lines that fall just below the knee. Empire silhouettes will make you look taller.
AVOID Very full skirts. Full-length hemlines can be too much "dress" for a petite frame. And keep embellishments to a minimum.

③ *full figure*

TRY A-line silhouettes. V-necks elongate your torso, and ruching, placed at the waist, imparts a nice, nipped-in look, and camouflages flaws.
AVOID Sheaths, mermaid styles—anything body-hugging.

(4) *generous bust*

TRY Scoop necks, V-necks, square necks, and halters that aren't too low-cut (too much cleavage is a no-no).

AVOID Bateau and Sabrina necklines.

(5) *hourglass figure*

TRY Retro silhouettes—think: Dior's "New Look" (a wasp waist and a full skirt). Or try the mermaid silhouette, which hugs curves in a smooth, sexy way and flares out at the hem.

AVOID "Straight" dresses and two-piece looks.

(6) *slim figure*

TRY Anything you like. If you're bony and want to create the illusion of curves, consider bias-cut gowns, and subtle draping at the bustline will make a small chest appear more shapely.

AVOID Boxy styles that hang on you, and too-tight sheaths or columns which can flatten you out and exaggerate your thinness.

satin, silk, or chiffon?

Your final consideration in the search for the perfect bridesmaid dress is the fabric, which will depend on the formality of the wedding, as well as the season, and time of day. Here are some of the options you might consider:

SATIN Shiny, princess-worthy, and luxe, it's the go-to black-tie fabric. Heavy satins should only be worn in fall and winter.

TAFFETA Luxurious, with an old-fashioned pedigree (it's what the ladies in *Vanity Fair* or *Anna Karenina* would wear to all those balls), the fabric has a subtle sheen and the most delicious rustle when you move around. Also, it's surprisingly lightweight, so you can wear it in any season.

TULLE If the bride has romantic visions of ballerinas, or winged fairies, you might end up wearing a dress of this delicate netting, perhaps peeking out as a petticoat. It's appropriate for any black-tie wedding.

SILK CHARMEUSE Supple, glamorous, and sexy, like lingerie. It's dressy enough for black-tie affairs, and can be worn in both the afternoon and evening. However, most girls find it difficult to wear—you need a perfect body!

CHIFFON It's popular for fancy summer celebrations and it's also brilliant for weddings on the beach because it's so light and airy.

ORGANZA A crisp, sheer, classic "evening dress" fabric that can be worn in the day or evening. Best for spring and summer weddings.

COTTON Plenty of bridesmaid dresses are fashioned of this ubiquitous fabric, from sheer, multi-layered cotton voile party dresses to seersucker and cotton piqué sheaths. Ideal for seashore or "smart casual" weddings in spring and summer (daytime affairs only).

VELVET Elegant, rich, sumptuous. Ideal for ultra-formal winter weddings.

SILK SHANTUNG There is simply no better fabric for bridesmaids to wear in an outdoor wedding. It displays the luster of fine silk, but with a nubby hand, so it's luxe, yet also understated.

CREPE The ultimate semiformal fabric, crepe can be worn in all seasons.

parties &
gifts

the bridal shower

The tradition of "showering" a bride with gifts harks back to a seventeenth century Dutch folk-tale. The story is as follows: In a small village, there was a girl who was set to marry a man who was decent, but poor—but her father didn't approve of the union and resolved to withhold his daughter's dowry if she went through with the wedding. In response to this threat, the girl's female friends rushed to her rescue with a stockpile of household items at the ready, including everything the girl would need to set up house

with her new husband. And the father was so touched by this generous show of love and support that he finally gave the marriage his blessing.

Hundreds of years later, it's still customary to fete the bride with a deluge of kitchen, bath, and bed essentials, as well as decorative pieces, for the new home she'll share with her husband. Contemporary brides also open gifts bearing trousseau items (think: frilly lingerie and satin nightgowns); "girlie" presents like bubble bath and personalized stationery are also quite common.

A bridesmaid should sit alongside the bride with pen and paper to record each gift, and the person who gave it.

Planning the shower is a collaborative effort split among the bridesmaids and family members close to the bride. The maid of honor is typically at the helm, and she may delegate tasks to bridesmaids, such as ordering the invitations or buying the party favors, refreshments, or decorations. Once everyone arrives, the pace of the party should be leisurely, and the atmosphere relaxed and intimate. The main activities at a bridal shower involve multi-generational girl-talk, nibbling on dainty pastries and hors d'oeuvres, and perhaps a parlor game or two. And the main event—watching the bride open her gifts.

getting it done

The idea that a bride's mother or other relative cannot officially host the bridal shower is an outdated notion. However, the maid of honor and her fellow bridesmaids still tend to host the bridal shower as a group. Here are some additional bridal shower conventions and planning guidelines:

TIMING The shower should take place about 4–6 weeks before the wedding (and shower invitations should be sent out 6–8 weeks prior to that date).

INVITATIONS Close friends and relatives usually comprise the guest list; consult the bride and her mother to find out who these people are if you do not know yourself. Anyone you invite to the shower must also be invited to the wedding.

LOCATIONS Bridal showers usually take place in a tea room or in a larger restaurant. Hosting an afternoon tea is popular because refreshments can be light, although bagel brunches and formal luncheons are also appropriate.

PARTY FAVORS Optional, but much appreciated.

The perfect party favor: scented soap (or another pretty toiletry item) with a note that reads: "From Helen's shower to yours…"

selecting a theme

A party that reflects a cohesive theme, from the invitations to refreshments and décor is always a success. For example, your theme might correspond to the bride's favorite color, or embrace a sophisticated Asian aesthetic. Gift-giving themes are also popular; be sure to type up a detailed explanation of your theme and enclose it with the invitations. Here are few classics:

RECIPE SHOWER Guests write out a favorite recipe on a recipe card and bring an item the bride would need to create or serve the recipe.

TIME OF DAY Guests are assigned a time of day and are asked to give a gift that pertains to that hour— a muffin tin (9am), a cocktail shaker or an ice bucket and tongs (5pm); silk pajamas (11pm).

ROOM OF THE HOUSE Assign guests rooms like, "dining room," "bedroom," "bathroom," "living room," and so on. This will net the bride a nice range of gifts, from china place settings to pillow shams and storage units.

modern alternatives

Many women find the traditional "just us girls" bridal shower to be a bit precious. Mature and remarrying brides may also find that the nature of a traditional bridal shower doesn't feel right. Your bride may wish to have a "Jack & Jill" shower instead, a party with a more grown-up, contemporary feel. Male and female guests are invited to a dinner party or cocktails at a club (a casual brunch or barbecue is fine, too). Gifts are gender-neutral, or point to one of the couple's shared interests, such as wine, travel, or sports.

If your bride isn't keen on having a Jack & Jill, you can still plan an intimate all-female gathering to wish her well. Consider a celebration that involves a special outing or group activity. Spend a Saturday afternoon taking a private guided shopping tour. Jewelry-making parties, held at a local bead shop, are also good fun. If the gang is into crafts, getting together to knit, scrap-book, or paint pottery may very well be the perfect solution. And a day at the spa will be delightful.

It's courteous to reference the groom on invitations to a female-only bridal shower.

gift ideas

The type of shower gift you give depends on the nature of the bride's personal style and interests. Here are suggestions for classic, artsy, athletic, and chic brides.

Traditional	Artistic
Monogrammed table linens	Handmade afghan or quilt
Crystal toasting flutes	Red wine glasses
Sterling hostess set	Letter opener
Toaster	Fondue pot
Silk peignoir	Caftan
Candlesticks	Incense burner
Vase	Sculpture

Sporty	Cosmopolitan
Beach towels	800 thread-count sheets
Pitcher and water tumblers	Martini glasses
Household tools	Chef's knife
Indoor grill	Espresso machine
White terrycloth robe	Designer lingerie
Flashlight	Luxe scented candles
Camera	Picture frames

the bachelorette party

A final, fabulous "girls' night out," while (hopefully) not as bawdy as a traditional bachelor party, is a tradition that many brides look forward to. Whether you dress up the bride in a boa and mini-veil and parade her around town for one night of mischief and merriment, or head out of town for a glamorous extravaganza that spans several days, here's what you need to know when planning the bachelorette party.

TIMING Most bachelorettes take place 2–4 weeks before the wedding.

INVITATIONS You needn't be formal (email is fine). Unlike the shower, you should feel free to invite anyone close to the bride, regardless of whether or not they're invited to the wedding.

ACTIVITIES Use your imagination. But karaoke or salsa dancing might be just as fun…

EXPENSES While bridesmaids are responsible for organizing the festivities, the total cost—including food, drinks, entertainment, and transportation—is split among all attendees.

*Hark, all you
ladies…the fairy
queen bids you
awake…You may
do in the dark what
the day doth forbid.
Fear not the dogs
that bark; night
will have all hid.*

THOMAS CAMPION

good clean fun

You know the bride best—if the usual bachelorette party hoopla definitely isn't her thing, don't force her to play along. There are plenty of sassy, classy ways to celebrate. You can all dress up and take in a show like *Cabaret* or *La Cage aux Folles*. Alternatively, you can go to a comedy club or attend a jazz concert; afterwards, lavish the bride with drinks and dessert at a posh café or lounge. Depending on your crowd, you can even plan a daytime activity, perhaps something outdoorsy like a day of sailing, or something more adventurous and exhilarating, like sky-diving or trapeze lessons.

Nowadays, bachelorette parties often occur within the context of a getaway to Las Vegas and other cities that tend to encourage all-out revelry. But your destination can be much more low-key—consider planning a leisurely weekend of wine-tastings in Napa or Sonoma County, or simply gather at someone's beach cottage to bond, play board games, and eat junk food.

If it makes more sense to gather locally, skip the clubs and organize a sumptuous catered dinner at someone's home. And a poker party might be the perfect alternative to carousing in an actual casino. Cheers!

etiquette
explained

Q. Do I have to buy the bride a wedding gift if she's having a destination wedding? On top of my dress, airfare, and accommodations, I'm spending way more than I can afford as it is.

A. Anyone invited to a wedding—including the bride's attendants—is obligated to give the couple a gift. While this may seem unfair, especially since you have put a strain on your finances just to participate in the wedding, keep in mind that one is only expected to give what one can reasonably afford. Your gift needn't be lavish (and it needn't be an item on her registry, either). To increase your buying power, save up those 25% off coupons that big-name department stores always seem to be offering; shop the housewares departments at off-price stores, which stock high-end brands at discounted price; and you'll also find, new, well-priced goods, from crystal to cutlery and appliances, at auction sites like ebay.com. You can also get away with spending very little cash if you give something unique and personal, like an assortment of Christmas ornaments or something exquisite and handmade that you purchase at a crafts fair, flea market, or gallery.

Q. One of my girlfriends was asked to devote an entire Saturday afternoon to stuffing and addressing invitations; another was expected to create centerpieces for the reception. These tasks seem above and beyond what a bridesmaid is supposed to do. Are they?

A. Stuffing invitations seems reasonable, although most bridesmaids are not asked to do this—brides tend to seek help from family members first. But creating centerpieces? That definitely not appropriate. Still, as a bridesmaid, it's your job to assist the bride—refusing to do a task is not an option. If you're faced with a "centerpiece" request (and you probably won't be), it's okay to voice your hesitation and concern, but don't speak up unless you can propose a solution, such as gently offering to help the bride find and hire an affordable florist.

Q. A "bridesmaids' luncheon" has been scheduled to take place during the wedding weekend. What is this event?

A. A quaint tradition that only a few brides honor, a bridesmaids' luncheon or tea is an intimate gathering—just some last-minute "girl time" to relax and enjoy a light meal together. Bridesmaid gifts are often presented at this time, too. After all you hard work, you deserve a celebration all your own.

Q. I'm my sister's maid of honor. We have a 12-year-old half-sister from our mother's second marriage and would like to include her in the bridal party. But she's certainly too old to be a flower girl. Is she too young to be a bridesmaid?

A. Your half-sister is the perfect age to be what's known as a junior bridesmaid (age 9 to 13). She should wear a demure version of the dress the bridesmaids will be wearing, as today's bridesmaid fashion tends to be quite sophisticated. Many bridesmaid dress designers have collections that are made specifically for the pre-teen set. For obvious reasons, junior bridesmaids are not held to the same financial obligations as adult bridesmaids (her parents usually pay for her attire). And since she's not of legal drinking age, it's not appropriate for a junior bridesmaid to attend a bachelorette party. However, when it comes to the bridal shower and just generally helping out, feel free to involve her in the planning and prep as much as possible. There are many small tasks that are just right for junior bridesmaids. For example, she can hand out programs as guests file into the ceremony. Afterward, she can distribute bubbles or rose petals to guests (for the couple's grand exit). At the reception, she can stand by the guest book and make sure everyone signs it. She can even help make decorations for the getaway car.

Q. The bride has asked me to give a toast at the reception. I don't know where to begin. How long should it be—and does it have to be funny?

A. Your speech should span no longer than two minutes. And no, your remarks needn't be humorous. However, they should certainly be thoughtful and heartfelt. Compose what you're going to say at least a week or two before the wedding. Start with a gracious "thank you" to the hosts of the wedding. Avoid talking about yourself (too many toastmasters do this when they're at a loss for words). Your remarks should simply include general good wishes for a happy future, a personal anecdote that everyone can relate to, and an inspiring take-home message about love and marriage (borrow from a book of quotations, if necessary). Conclude by raising your glass of champagne and saying "To Samantha and Thomas!"

If the best man is also making a toast, discuss the nature of your speeches in advance to determine who should take the microphone first (it's best if funny precedes sentimental). And remember, you don't have to memorize your toast; it's perfectly acceptable to read from note cards. Just make sure you're comfortable and that the words flow easily from your lips—practice makes perfect!

Q. I'm pregnant and will be very pregnant when the bride's wedding rolls around. Will she still want me to be in her wedding?

A. Of course! As long as you're having an easy time of it, there's no reason why you can't fulfill your bridesmaid responsibilities. As for the dress, you'll have to get a maternity version and you'll be pleased to know that many big-name bridesmaid dress designers offer styles that are friendly to growing bellies (an empire waist is your best bet). To make sure you get the most accurate fit, order a size larger than you think you're going to need and have it tailored as close to the wedding date as possible.

Q. The bride has chosen a pair of black peau-de-soie shoes she'd like us to wear. They cost $120, and I already own a pair of shoes that are quite similar. Do I have to buy these new ones?

A. The simple answer is—yes. If she allows you this substitution, the other girls may become resentful and/or ask for similar allowances, and that puts the bride in an awkward situation. However, it doesn't hurt to ask. She may be more flexible if your bridesmaid dress is long, in which case the shoes won't really show.

picture credits

All photographs by Winfried Heinze unless otherwise stated below:
Claire Richardson page 5 above center, 44 above left, 46, 50, 51, 52;
Polly Wreford pages 17, 54–55, 64; Craig Fordham page 2;
Sandra Lane page 44 below right; Ian Wallace pages 48–49.
Make-up by Marie Keaveney-Allen

The author and publisher would like to thank the following for lending
us beautiful dresses and accessories:

JLM Europe Ltd.
tel: 0800 3281531
www.jlmeurope.co.uk

Berketex Bride
www.bbride.com

Debenhams
www.debenhams.com

VV Rouleaux
6 Marylebone High Street
London W1M 3PB
UK
www.vvrouleaux.com

acknowledgments

The author would like to dedicate this book to all bridesmaids everywhere—past, present, and future. She would also like to thank Alison, Miriam, Sonya, and everyone at Ryland Peters & Small.